The Heart Of Rel Connectic

A Modern Guide To Master The Art Of Relationship Communication, Self-Development And Connect Better In Your Relationships

John T. Collins PsyD & Rachel Collins MD

Copyright 2021 - All rights reserved.

Table Of Contents

Introduction.. 8

Chapter 1.   Stress Management 10

Learn to Tolerate your Emotions 12

Distract Yourself from Negative Emotions....................................... 15

Change Your Behavior 18

Become Aware of your Behavior 18

Do the Opposite 19

Chapter 2.   Develop Together 22

Chapter 3.   Learn to Apologize in a Conscious Way 32

The Way to Build This Habit.. 38

In What Ways Are You Holding Back? 39

Pick the Least Difficult Topic to Start Your Practice. 39

Since the Listener, Enable Your Spouse to Become Direct
Without Responding. 40

Request What You Need, Not Everything You Do Not Want. 41

As Your Listener, Represent, Affirm, and Request More. 42

Since the Listener, Confirm Again and Again Answer. 42

Chapter 4.   Learn to Forgive in a Conscious Way 44

Chapter 5.   Accepting Criticism.. 57

When You Are Dealing With Criticism in Relationships:.......... 58

Some Thoughts on Constructive Criticism 60

The Art of Criticizing and Getting Rid of the Bad Feelings
Successfully.. 61

Chapter 6.   Trust Your Partner.. 63

Chapter 7.   Revive Your Sex Life 71

Maintain Physical Contact and Affection 72

Educate Yourself.. 72

Make Time for Sex 73

Discuss Your Sexual Fantasies 74

Communicate During Sex.. 74

Relax 75

Practice the Sensate Focus Technique............................ 75

Chapter 8.   Love.. 81

Use Affirmations 85

Make Your Spouse Feel Important................................. 87

Chapter 9.   Accept Your Partner.................................... 92

Chapter 10. Communicate with Your Partner 102

Communication Is Not Just Verbal................................ 103

Facial Expressions.. 105

Paralinguistic Communication.. 106

Body Posture 107

Causes of Miscommunication in a Relationship........... 108

CONCLUSION... 112

Introduction

Imagine you have met him—he seems perfect. He is charming, funny, and seems entirely interested in listening to you. He brings you gifts months later that are related to little conversations that you have had before, such as bringing you that newly-in-season drink you had mentioned months prior. He seems like a great guy—until it seems like a light turned off. The man who once was kind and caring, attentive, and aware, suddenly is demanding. You find yourself shifting from feeling like you were adored when you first met to feeling constantly guilty. You feel like you can't do anything right when he's around, and just the sight of him can be enough for you to feel like you cannot breathe. You are miserable—in love, desperately so, but you cannot deny that the love that you are feeling is also incredibly painful.

This man, even with the little given, is showing tendencies of narcissism. The proverbial you in that story is showing the telltale signs of narcissistic abuse—feeling madly in love, but like the love that is felt is miserable, draining, and painful.

Chapter 1.   Stress Management

When our insecurities are triggered, what we feel is emotional pain. This emotional pain is responsible for our actions. We react to it, and it makes us behave in unhelpful ways that will only add up to already existing emotional pain. No matter how hard you try, you can't get rid of your negative emotions and thoughts. They always keep reemerging. Just like with behavior and thoughts, you need to learn how to manage your emotions properly. You need to learn how to accept them for what they are even though they are the main reason why you feel the pain.

When your emotions manifest due to your insecurities, you feel pain and you start remembering the situation that caused the insecurity. You start reliving the past, either through your memories or just by feeling the same as you did back then. This will make you blind to the fact that you are in the present and in a different situation. Your behavior will reflect your insecurities, and they will be unhelpful and harm you even more.

Learn to Tolerate your Emotions

There are three main reasons why your emotions keep reappearing:

1.   Rumination: when you keep thinking about your past painful experience that caused your insecurity. You won't let go of it and you keep returning to it over and over again.

2.   Avoidance: When you don't face your emotions, you keep putting them off. You do not allow yourself to experience your emotions and you can't accept them.

3.   Behavior: If your emotions cause you to behave in harmful ways, your emotions will keep coming back even stronger or they will now be caused by your behavior that is endangering your relationship.

What you need to do when your emotions appear is choose the reaction that will not keep hurting you; it won't make you or your partner feel bad, and it won't damage your current relationship. Let's observe what happens with emotions when our insecurity is triggered: once the situation presents itself and you feel at your worst, your emotions are very painful, overwhelming, and you can't bear to feel that way.

It is quite normal to want to get rid of them as soon as possible so why should you endure the pain? You start behaving in unnatural ways, ways that are against your own core values. This is why you feel even worse after you let your emotions cause unhelpful behavior. Sometimes these behaviors will make you feel better in the short term, but in the long term, emotions will be back and will strike you even harder.

Emotions are unavoidable, and there is nothing you can do not to feel. What you can control in this situation is a response to your negative emotions. Don't allow them to control your behavior. You are the only one who should have the full control. Accept the responsibility of the way you feel, and don't give in. Adopt behaviors that are healthy and that won't have suffering as a consequence. This is exactly the part you can avoid, the suffering. It is pretty simple. Due to your own insecurity you might want to withdraw socially and disconnect from others completely. As a consequence, this will mean you will miss the opportunity of having good experiences. In time, you will lose your friends, and you will feel lonely and depressed. This is when suffering becomes intolerable. What you need to do is fight your urge to withdraw and close up. You need to allow yourself to feel the emotion but not to give in to it. It has no control over it. You are the one who will decide how to behave in situations that trigger your insecurity. Instead of missing out on friends and good experiences, it's better to join them and cope with your insecurity surrounded with friends who will offer you support. You will not suffer this way.

Distract Yourself from Negative Emotions

If you are afraid that negative emotions are going to overwhelm you and you won't be able to tolerate them, or take control of your behaviors, there is an option of distracting yourself. Be sure to use only healthy distraction activities; this means engage yourself in any helpful and healthy activity that will divert you from the negative emotions you are feeling.

Distracting yourself from emotions will create a window of time that will allow emotions to decrease, and there will be no reason to react on them anymore. The behavior you would execute to feel better will no longer be needed. With your emotions still present, but with lower intensity, you will be cold headed enough to make smart decisions, even observe them objectively, and make proper choices on how to react.

When you distract yourself from negative and hurtful emotions, it doesn't mean you are trying to ignore or forget about them. It is about giving yourself time to clear your head so you can approach the insecurity that caused emotions in the first place with rationality and logic. There are plenty of activities you can partake to distract yourself from strong, negative emotions:

Exercising: We do not need to mention the health benefits of exercising. It influences your whole body in a positive way. It will help you to lose weight, it will improve oxygen flow and help with elevated blood pressure. Be sure that you choose an exercise that is to your liking. We are not all capable of doing extreme sports no matter how much we want. Start with some light exercises. Even dancing can be a good exercise that will distract you from your emotions.

Hobbies: Another activity that will distract you is engaging in hobbies. It can be anything you want and find interesting. Identify activities you find interesting to and don't wait. Start doing it now. We are often lazy about our hobbies, thinking there is never enough time and there are always more important things to do. Stop thinking like that; hobbies are great way to entertain yourself and stay distracted when needed. It can be anything you find interesting: photography, learning how to play an instrument, cooking, knitting. The possibilities are endless.

Volunteering: Earlier in this book we learned that volunteering is about having a purpose or a task that goes beyond you and your own needs. Helping others puts focus on a good cause that will distract you from what you feel. It also feels rewarding to help someone else. If you want, you can join big organizations that will help you decide how best to spend your time volunteering with the programs they offer or you could do simple stuff such as helping your elderly neighbor shop or walk his dog on a daily basis. It doesn't have to be anything grand. The main thing is to move the focus from yourself to someone else. It will make you feel good about yourself in the most unselfish way.

Tasks: Another great way to distract yourself is to do the tasks you were putting off finally. Especially if you feel stressed under the pressure of emotions. Begin a project you meant to finish but never had the time. Clean the house, build shelves, organize your books, paint your home, do regular house chores. It will also give you needed exercise, and physical work will count. It will release endorphins that will combat your stress and help you feel better about yourself.

Change Your Behavior

We tackled how it is impossible to change your core beliefs. You can't change your emotions that are product of your insecurities, but you can change the way you behave to answer those emotions and core beliefs. There are two things you need to do so you can manage to change your behavior successfully: Be aware of your current behavior and how it influences your relationship and do the opposite.

Become Aware of your Behavior

Our behaviors that come from insecurities are nothing more than patterns that we must break in order to change the influence of insecurity on our relationship. If you look back on your past behaviors, you will get the best possible chance to change them in future. Don't be ashamed of your past behaviors, and don't think of them as something bad. They were unhelpful, for sure, and that is the only term we need to be aware of. Now we want to change our behaviors to helpful.

Do the Opposite

It will take a lot of energy to resist old habits and change your behavior to helpful ones, but as you practice and access new adopted behaviors, it will become easier. At one point, it will come without effort, almost automatically and naturally. This will make you feel better about yourself; it will be a great accomplishment. Instead of feeling unworthy, you will start to boost your self-esteem. Even your partner will recognize your effort and will reward you with even more love.

If you see and feel that all your former behaviors didn't work, then it's only logical to do the opposite and see how that ends up. But what would the opposite be? First, let's look at some usual responses and behaviors you might have.

For example, you have abandonment insecurity and emotional deprivation core belief. You are dating your partner and you really like him. A situation happens at work that triggers your insecurities and you need reassurance; it's only natural to seek it from your partner. You call him, but he doesn't answer. You call him three more times to no avail. You start thinking that he doesn't like you as much as you like him; he is going to leave you, otherwise he would answer the phone. You start feeling anxious, depressed and scared, and you are already hurting. You have a strong urge to find out why isn't he answering right away and you keep calling. He finally answers the phone; he is in panic and asks what's wrong. You explain it's nothing, just your job and your need to hear his voice. He then informs you that he was in the middle of meeting with an important client and your constant calling disrupted it. He hangs up. You feel bad about the situation and text him asking for forgiveness and say you panicked, and it is not your usual behavior. But it is it is the behavior pattern you have when you feel insecure. Soon enough, your partner will have enough and will want out of the relationship.

Now we can break down your behavior from past experience and see how we can turn an unhelpful behavioral pattern into a helpful pattern.

1.   You seek unnecessary communication.

2.   You need reassurance.

3.   You are clingy.

4.   You are in need for certainty.

This would be helpful, opposite behavior:

1.   Do not initiate communication and if you must, be sure you are not intruding on your partner's privacy.

Instead, pick up a distracting behavior. It can involve hobby, a quick exercise or simply organize your work desk.

Chapter 2.   Develop Together

You should make it your priority to evolve together, expecting each other in difficult times continually. Good communication is the key when it comes to growing together. Good communication involves spouses showing each other that they are listening. Having a conversation with someone who is utterly quiet can make one feel that they are conversing with themselves.

It is, therefore, important that every spouse contributes to show they are listening. For example, a spouse may add on to what the other person has said. This shows that everyone is listening attentively and processing the issues. If, for example, one person is talking about their day at work, the partner may say, "It sounds as if that office has some people with personal issuers rubbing off on everybody. The things that the secretary said would tick me off too". The person may also add "What can I do to make your day better." Language like this shows a partner that they have been understood and that they can get help if they need it.

Good communication is not all about talking and talking. Sometimes, the best medicine involves a good level of silence. For instance, when two people are having a conversation, they can take a break to digest what they have said to each other. The silence will help the two people put their thoughts in order and avoid blunting out things unintentionally. Open communication and conversation do not mean going on and on in an endless conversation. Take a break and a breath. Good silence also indicates to the partners that they are reflecting on all that has been said.

Good and open communication requires one to be sensitive to the moods, schedules, and other factors of their partner. Select a good time to have an effective back and forth based on the conversation you want to have. However, things that need to be addressed should not be ousted too far off. Address matters openly as soon as possible because dwelling on them in silence will bring problems. One should pick a suitable moment as soon as possible and open up.

Another important factor that can help couples grow together is honoring the opinions of a partner even if they differ. Honoring different views is one of the main keys to good communication. To show honor of different opinions, one may say "I understand what you are saying, but I think... Can we agree to disagree?" Such statements will not only acknowledge that one person has understood the other but also that they respect a different opinion. They also help one state their different opinion without overstepping their boundaries. Honoring the views of each other de-escalates what could have become a conflict.

Couples need to identify ways of having the most productive conversations which will add value to their marriage. One of the best ways of maintaining an emotional connection is through holding good open conversations. Couples should segregate time to hold conversations and put some of the tips named above into practice.

The importance of practicing day after day to achieve a mindful relationship

Communication in marriage and connection are directly related. Without one, the other is likely to fail. When people can express themselves adequately, things tend to be better even when they cannot agree on a particular subject. For instance, if a couple is talking about how much money they should spend on entertainment per month, the husband may want more to go to movies and games while the wife wants more to go with her girlfriends for shopping sprees. The couple may not initially agree on the amount they should spend, but so long as they are communicating about it, they both understand what the other wants. When communication is a challenge, one may feel that the other is being wasteful and still not express it in the right way. Bad communication leads to feelings of isolation, sadness, loneliness, heartbroken and disheartened.

Communication is important for both simple and tough reasons. In the movies, couples seem to have some almost perfect lives, but in the real world, it is more complicated than that. People have to make decisions about children, money, work life, obligations, and other action items without a screen script to follow. Such matters call on the couples to have deep conversations. Even the little things that could be ignored before the couple lives together have to be taken into consideration; otherwise, the marriage might fail. Without the right communication in marriage, drifts happen, and the couple that was ones so in love becomes strangers sharing a table. Again, communication in marriage differs from communication in a relationship because couples tend to get tired of the masks want to deal with real feelings. The spouses want to be heard; their deep needs start to surface; they want to be validated. If one person keeps dismissing, interrupting or shutting down their partner, there will be a rift between them.

Good communication leads to a great marriage and more. As seen earlier, communication and connection go together and consequently if one goes down, the other fails too. Every couple should strive to revive the communication whenever there are hiccups because it will lead to stronger intimacy both physically and emotionally. Communication is not required in marriage just for emotional and physical connection. The couples also need to make decisions about development and growth.

In many cases, development and growth involve making decisions about money. When two people come together in marriage, there are a lot of emotions that get tied up in how they spend money. If therefore the couple keeps pushing aside conversations about money decisions, a lot of problems will arise soon in the family. Communication is also important because people only have a finite amount of time on earth- no one wants to be in a relationship where there is no connection. That is why many people opt for divorces when the spouses are no longer connected. One way to avoid separations and stay connected for a long time is to keep rediscovering things about one another more so through communication. Change for the better and show it to one another that you are putting effort to make it work. Share experiences create new memories which you can discuss later and laugh. Good communication ensures that the couple knows which statements would make the other person shut down or build a wall; therefore, they avoid offending one another. Good communication is proactive such that, instead of waiting for things to go wrong to start a conversation, the couple sorts things out in time. The results of good communication are a solid foundation in the marriage where the couple can talk about anything without fear.

Many couples who have difficulties in communication think that it will take an arm and a leg to get back on track. Although this might be true for some broken communications, the majority of the couples need to make small steps towards better communication, and they will achieve a considerable difference. A few adjustments to the channels of communication and the spouses will achieve a tremendous compounding effect on their relationship and marriage. While facing communication challenges, many couples also tend to feel like they are the only ones undergoing this. It is important for them to remember that they are not the only ones facing challenges. Challenges are normal in every relationship. The key to solving the problems is consistency.

Remember, a distance between couples or any two people does not happen overnight. There is not just one reason which leads to a total drift in a couple that was once madly in love. It is a result of small omissions and commissions that offend the other person, therefore, creating mountains of differences and gaps between the two people. In the initial stages of a relationship and marriage, a couple can easily thrive on excitement and physical attraction, therefore, communication plays a small role and many of its aspects will be ignored.

As the bond between the two individuals deepens, the attraction changes very fast into the first stages of love where every person is making a foundation of trust. This is because they want to have a stronger and happier future. When in marriage, the love that once thrived on attraction and excitement changes to one that is sustained by trust, commitment, and honesty. Over the years, the responsibilities change, and the amount of stress increases with an increase in challenges. Somehow, the time to be there for one another and to share seems to diminish.

Communication becomes a chore that couples would rather skip even if it is talking about a joyous moment. Things seem to change, and the couples that thought marriage is a completely smooth ride usually feel cheated or lost. The suppressed negative feelings that arise from this situation make a couple preys to miscommunication or total lack of it. Then the drift occurs, followed by assumption and mistrusts, in worse cases infidelity, lack of respect, dishonesty, et cetera.

Good communication means that a couple respects one another enough to stay honest.

Demystifying the fairytales

In all healthy relationships, communication must act as the centerpiece. All individuals in all relationships whether in marriage or workplace must maintain good communication and check in regularly. Marriages consist of more than just keeping a household, parenting and taking care of bills. With time, the couple begins to understand that the fairy tale-happily ever after has many holes and it takes a lot of effort from both sides to make it work.

In real life, knights on horses rarely ride in and rescue damsels in distress to a happily ever after situation. Consequently, it is important for spouses to remember to talk to one another rather than at each other. Married Couples are in a full-time job called marriage where they should always love and appreciate each other to achieve their marriage goals. The difficult part is that most of the spouses in marriages do not know how to alter their mentality to accommodate real life things that make marriages work. That is why when many couples have difficulties communicating;

they focus on the divorce statistics and the number of maintenance cases in the courts. When the spouses realize that the number of cases is too high, they get into panic mode and set the same expectations for their own homes. This expectations and standards tend to kill the marriages that would otherwise thrive.

It is wrong for people to use what is happening around them to gauge their marriages. Most of the statists given to the public only involve detrimental unions. They hardly tell people of the winning marriages and how they got there. In other words, those offering statistics to the public do not tell them what it takes for the marriages to fail or succeed. They fail to discuss the satisfaction levels and communication in marriages, and therefore people do not realize that most marriages fail because of things that would be solved through communication.

Chapter 3.   Learn to Apologize in a Conscious Way

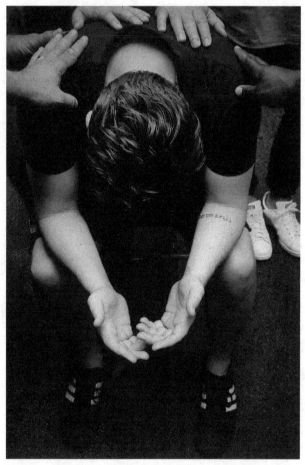

Are you and your partner able to become leaders with you another, conveying your needs and demands without nervousness, jealousy, or distress? Or do you end up holding back or with more passive methods for communicating your requirements? Since nobody wants to battle or suffering, we occasionally skirt about problems, vaguely indicating what we desire without saying precisely what we mean. Some people confuse being led with being rude or rough; thus, we're reticent to talk for fear of breaking. Or some people fear rejection or put-downs in their spouse when they speak upright and discuss their ideas and feelings. If a subject is awkward or emotionally charged, we could return from the urge to prevent uncomfortable, embarrassing confrontations. And then there are the instances we believe our spouse should examine our heads and only intuit what we need without us needing to inform them.

We correlate love with brain reading, and it is a set up for bitterness and unhappiness. Some individuals have a harder time putting their feelings into words or words, just what they want since they have not taken the opportunity to self-reflect and comprehend their particular requirements and passions. Being developed adults (along with a nutritious couple) requires both spouses to state what they believe, request what they want, and also express themselves publicly --with kindness and confidence. Additionally, it requires both spouses to react to direct communicating without defensiveness, fearing, criticism, or anger.

When you talk right to your spouse, your speech is clear, simple, and unambiguous. There's not any pretense or a hidden message from direct communication; its objective is very just to get or provide information and start a dialog with your spouse. It includes the two way, free-flowing sharing of ideas, emotions, and thoughts in a manner that contributes to options. You'd think this could be simple, and for a few, it's. However, the majority of us have difficulty communicating right in some places of our connection; thus, we resort to all kinds of verbal communication to be able to express ourselves. Or we brush up our feelings till they float and melt in unproductive ways.

Let's take a look at a few of the ways that you may not be communicating right on your relationship and what you could do about this. You sign, want, and expect without saying what you mean. Let us say you have had a particularly stressful day, and you are beginning to develop a cold. It is the turn to prepare dinner; however, you genuinely don't feel like that. So, you say to a spouse, "Boy, I feel like a truck hit on me, but I figure I want to begin fixing supper." What you mean is, "Honey, I'm not feeling well. Can you please fix supper tonight, and I will pick up the idle next week" With

34

the first announcement, you sign at issue but not directly request a solution?

Leaving vague hints regarding what you need is passive and does not always lead to your spouse catching on to a significance. Save yourself and your spouse time and psychological energy from cutting to the chase in the first area and saying what you want.

You may also end up hoping and wishing to get something out of your spouse without realizing it. You hope he'll see just how much you want a hug. You want her to initiate sex more frequently. However, from distress or even the false belief that your spouse ought to be a mind reader, so your own emotions move unvoiced. Should you wish and hope to everything you need without mentioning it, then the chances are slim, your preferences will be contemplated. You've got to take personal responsibility for saying what you need in a means that's thoughtful but apparent to your spouse.

You wonder, suppose, and suppose without asking. A number of the worst struggles in relationships will be the result of speculating and reacting to your premises. You see, your partner is becoming silent, and you finish. He is angry at you. You assume that your spouse does not wish to go to the pictures with you personally, but you fail to ask. You wonder why the boyfriend does not enjoy holding hands in public, and that means you assume he is losing interest. When you feel like this, you're feeling helpless and confused. You also set the platform for misunderstandings and disagreements. Perhaps you have said something for your spouse enjoy, "You sounded angry at me, so I assumed that you did not wish to venture out," just to have your spouse say, "What exactly are you speaking about? I never stated I was angry. I truly wished to go out," We frequently produce stories in our minds about what our spouse is feeling or thinking, or what their goals may be.

Despite somebody we all know well; we do not always understand what they mean or how they will respond. If you'd like clarity and reassurance, inquire. Do not just assume, imagine, and also wonder. Asking also proves that you honor your spouse enough to affirm what is in their thoughts and their center. Attempt using open-ended questions that encourage complete disclosure as opposed to yes or no questions according to your guess or premise. So instead of saying, "Are you angry at me for a reason" You may say, "Do you feel about our link at this time?" Rather than saying, "I imagine you do not wish to go to the pictures tonight," you'd say, "What would you feel like doing tonight?" Another manner of becoming direct on your communication is by saying what you do not need rather than what you want. Framing an announcement for your spouse together with the negative term, "I do not desire," is placing them to the defensive until you complete uttering this sentence. It contributes to negativity instead of clarity. Consider the difference in Both of These paragraphs and how you'd respond to them:

- "I do not need the parents to come on Sunday."

- "I want to invest Sunday carrying a rise together and using brunch."

The next announcement invites a more favorable reply and provides more information for your spouse. Additionally, it boosts the chance for a dialog instead of throwing up a roadblock. Becoming directly with your spouse might feel uneasy in specific scenarios. If you're more likely to talk, it may take a while to build up this habit. But speaking in a means that's positive, clear, and type shows your spouse that you honor yourself, and you appreciate your connection sufficient to say what you mean. Maintaining back and forth being obscure may seem safer in the brief term; however, it does not serve the long term aims of good honesty and communication in your connection.

The Way to Build This Habit

You're able to practice the custom of becoming more direct in your communication by practicing dialogues by that you and your spouse share in requesting something which you need or need from another. Put aside some time at the start of the week to get the conversation for sharing your requirements. All these dialogues will feel stilted and unnatural at first, but with practice, you'll have the ability to use a conversational style that suits you as a few. The objective of every phrase in the dialog "script" will be to help keep you on course so that the dialogue does not devolve. Adhering to this script will Permit You to listen more empathically to another and achieve a settlement more quickly.

In What Ways Are You Holding Back?

Contemplate some unmet demands or requests you've got for your spouse, which you haven't expressed from anxiety or distress. These may be topics you have attempted to show or indirectly; however, your spouse has not gotten the concept. Create a list of whatever springs to mind.

Pick the Least Difficult Topic to Start Your Practice.

If you have trouble becoming a guide, you might not wish to begin this habit clinic with the subject that makes one of the most embarrassing. Make your feet wet using a question you can talk without an excessive amount of stress. As you construct your confidence speaking right, you can tackle more challenging issues.

Since the Listener, Enable Your Spouse to Become Direct Without Responding.

One reason people are not direct is simply that they fear the way their spouse will respond. It is tough to be forthright if you stress your spouse is going to be angry, defensive probably, or even hurt. As you practice creating direct statements and asks, you need to pay attention without crime or anger as soon as your spouse makes her or his statement. It can be tough to listen to something which reflects a weakness or which activates fear or unhappiness, but you have to learn how to listen to your spouse's requirements without revealing negative responses. Bear in mind, and it's also difficult for your spouse to be more direct with you and thus doesn't make it more robust by responding poorly. You'll have time throughout the dialog to show your emotions and responses mindfully as soon as you've listened to a spouse. Hopefully, through this addiction clinic, both you and your spouse are going to discover to exhibit your requirements directly but additionally with kindness and compassion.

Request What You Need, Not Everything You Do Not Want.

Bear in mind that has a requirement or want, therefore, state what that's in favorable words, instead of telling your spouse what he or she wants to quit doing or to alter. State your desire or want succinctly, right, and wholeheartedly using "I" statements. It's simpler just to get out the words with no buildup, qualifiers, or hemming and hawing.

•   "I'd like us to exercise together so we could lose weight."

•   "I want your presence at my family reunion."

•   "I would prefer for us to proceed to marriage counseling together."

•   "I want your help getting dinner on the table tonight."

As Your Listener, Represent, Affirm, and Request More.

Whenever your spouse creates an immediate statement about a demand, mirror the announcement and affirm that you heard it correctly. "You want me to join for the family reunion. Is that right?" If you noticed your spouse correctly, ask your spouse if he or she has to discuss by stating, "Can there be more?"

Since the Listener, Confirm Again and Again Answer.

Yet more, mirror what you've heard your spouse request, inquiring if you noticed it properly. Then affirm that you know the reason why this petition is significant to your spouse.

Chapter 4.   Learn to Forgive in a Conscious Way

When you first get into a relationship, it seems impossible that the two of you will ever fight or argue about anything at all. Everything seems perfect, and there couldn't be a better person for you than them. However, boom, as the relationship progresses, you have the first real fight that catches you totally off guard. It feels like your near perfect world has comes crashing down. Rest assured that it is normal to have arguments even in the early stages of your relationship unless it's a major deal-breaker or something that is unlawful or poses a threat to your safety.

Approach your first disagreement or argument with a clear game plan to survive choppy waters and ensure smooth sailing in the long run. Is it not a thorough waste of energy, time and opportunity to let a single argument destroy the foundation of your relationship? Here are some powerful pointers to handle your first big argument or disagreement during the courtship or dating phase.

1.   Don't Think in Extremes

Now highlight this if you want to in another color but just because you've had an argument or disagreement doesn't really mean all the love and affection has evaporated into thin air suddenly. You are a couple not a pair of conjoined twins (even they have fights for god's sake). There are bound to be differences and disagreements as long as you keep it healthy. Don't jump to the worst conclusion or speak things you'll later regret. Sometimes, we say things in the heat of the moment, without meaning them. Avoid doing this.

Don't immediately say things such as, "We should consider ending the relationship" or "let's just call it off" or "I hate your attitude." One of the best signs of a healthy relationship is that both the partners have emotions that aren't dependent on then agreeing with each other. You'll have to learn to handle the differences through the fights. Avoid jumping to the worst conclusion or catastrophizing the fight. Remember, there are several other complex factors that determine if you are a good fit as a couple rather than letting minor issues that wreak havoc. Don't take your eyes off the bigger picture.

The worst you can do when it comes to your first fight as a couple is overreacting. It can tip off a small tiff into a full-fledged fight. Ask yourself these questions when you have your first fight or disagreement as a couple. "Did I or my partner get too emotional?" This is important information as one must figure out who out of the two (or both) have a more drama-focused style or extreme emotions.

If you are the drama prone partner, opt for therapy or take the help of self-help books to manage your emotions better. If it is another person, you may want to talk to them and honestly ask if this is a habitual pattern, they need help with. While some people are psychologically equipped to handle high emotion partners, but there aren't suitable for everyone. Know your tolerance level before moving ahead slowly.

2.   Don't Hold Grudges

The first thing you can do during the courtship phase of your relationship is to hold grudges against your partner long after the first big after is done and dusted. It doesn't reflect well on you. You know how it feels when someone won't say something during a fight and years later make you feel miserable about it? You feel you are being crucified for something that you didn't even realize. Don't do it with your partner. Don't be the person that holds grudges about arguments and disagreements that happened years ago.

Don't use your couple arguments as ammunitions for scoring future 'wins.' Don't make it a cause for a future break-up, to win new fights or to induce guilt within the partner (manipulate them into giving you what you what). It makes you come across as a highly nasty and calculative person or reveals larger issues between you both as a couple. Let to let go of trivial issues, disagreements and differences.

You will have disagreements all the time in a relationship because you are two different individuals with minds of your

47

own. As long the issues you disagree on aren't huge, learn to navigate your way through the differences. Reading more into tiny differences will add more negativity to the relationship.

When you forgive, forgive forever. Couple fights are not battlegrounds. Once the Great Home Cleaning Battle of 2017 is done, it shouldn't be raised again. Even if there's a Great Home Cleaning Battle of 2018, the earlier one shouldn't be brought up. Holding on hurtful and angry words of the past only leads to greater anger and hurt. Don't let the wounds of past arguments fester. Once you forgive, look forward towards a happy future.

3.   Give The Person Space

Funny as it sounds; every couple has a distinct way of fighting and arguing. You may take a long time to understand what your disagreement approach as a couple is. For example, some folks are quick to go all nails and daggers on each other. Do some emotional digging to find out to find out what is truly bothering your partner. Give each other space and time to understand what has happened and figure out your subsequent moves. Call a time out on the argument rather than letting it linger around.

Also be honest. Attempt to say something like, "Well thinking about the disagreement we had, I was upset because I'd really like you to do this since it will help our relationships in XYZ ways." You are saying what you want without sounding accusatory and putting your partner on the defensive. Ensure that you give more time to the relationship before jumping to what the fight implies for your new relationship. At times, you realize that you'd simply be overreacting.

4.   Use It to Set Ground Rules For Future Fights

Once you've had your first fight, take some time to breathe easy, let in sink in and relax. Take a few minutes to tell your partner what that you want to go over some ground rules for future disagreements and fights. Recognize what is acceptable and what is not acceptable during arguments. For example, if you just can't stand someone yelling, tell them straight off. Similarly, if you don't thrive on emotional drama, make it clear to the partner. There are some things that are beyond your scope of acceptance. Talk about them to your partner. Similarly, let him or her share about their non-negotiators too.

5.   Understand All Happy Couples Argue

It is funny how so many people live with the misconception that happy couples seldom fight or have disagreements. For god's sake, healthy and happy couples have differences. The frequency of a couple's fight is not an indicator of the relationship; it is the intensity that reveals where your relationship stands.

Disagreeing in a healthy, respectful manner for a short while without blowing it up into a full-blown war is fine. The couple can get annoyed, exasperated or frustrated. However, as long as you can talk about your feelings or they don't reach an extreme level, you are doing fine.

6.   Attempt To Diffuse the Situation Using Facts

Don't let your first or even future fights be about gossip, assumptions, guesswork and rumors. Avoid letting meaningless drama hold center stage. One of the best ground rules you can set a couple is to stick to facts during disagreements or arguments. This doesn't mean you shouldn't say how you feel. It just means, there is an appropriate way to communicate exactly how you feel. However, there is a stark difference between expressing emotion and accusing or attacking the other person. Don't cross that line!

7.   Don't Issue Ultimatums

We may not issue black and white ultimatums. However, they get more subtle over a period of time. They may no longer be threats but artfully positioned. The other person doesn't even realize that an ultimatum is being issued to them. "I think we should just break-up." This is an ultimatum, even though it's subtle.

If your partner issues these ultimatums, tell them that it's disrespectful towards you or the relationship. Ask them to refrain from making impulsive decisions. If they realize that they should respectful towards the relationship, forgive them and move on. Let them not use the relationship as collateral to score a victory. If they are using it to win the argument, it's a huge red flag. They may keep doing it all the time.

8.   Keep Fights Clean

It may not always be simple to keep it clean, especially when you are seething with rage. Plus, there's no referee to moderate the fight. However strong the urge, never hit below the belt! It will lay the foundation for an unhealthy and destructive relationship. Work hard to maintain respect and an element of positivity even during fights. Keep your name calling, accusations, bad language and personal attacks in check. State facts and how something makes you feel.

If the other person gets dirty or nasty, calmly and assertively tell them that they are crossing the limit. The objective should be to emerge from the disagreement as a stronger, more matured and wiser person rather than more resentful.

Fighting dirty or hitting below the belt can be more gratifying than resorting to a clean fight. However, it damages your relationship in the long run. It can be anything from hurling hurtful accusations or insults that are you or your partner don't really mean. Don't aggravate your partner by adding insult to injury.

9. Save Conflict Resolution for Face-to-face Communication

Choose to never fight over text messages, social media and calls. Always attempt to resolve arguments face-to-face, where you can communicate through powerful non-verbal signals as well. If it is about an issue that is deeply disturbing or emotionally draining, you need to discuss it with your partner face-to-face. There shouldn't be any scope for miscommunication and misinterpretation over emojis, weird text or unspoken words. Take the guesswork and assumption out of communication. If things are not clear, ask for further clarification in calm and composed manner.

10.   Have a Game Plan Ready to Handle Miscommunication?

Does your partner lash out at you during an argument or get nasty? Do they resort to the silent treatment? Is there a tendency to get irritatingly clingy and nagging? Do they get mad at you and say hurtful things? Your first fight as a couple is a good time to weed out folks who become increasingly angry hit below the belt or are immature to handle.

Judge the other person's style of fighting without making sweeping statements or generalizations. Also, understand that your partner is judging your style. So, keep it fair and healthy.

Chapter 5.   Accepting Criticism

Criticism is a serious concern for many people, and worse, people are concerned with criticizing others because they fear being criticized themselves. Sometimes it's a terrible feeling, mainly if it's done viciously.

The fact is, having critical feedback can also be a positive thing and a crucial part of a healthy relationship. However, in a bad relationship, a relation may deteriorate and separate partners, mainly if the criticism is continuous and excessive.

Criticizing might make or break a relationship, depending on whether it's done correctly or used as a tool.

There are a few guidelines that you can follow if you want things to improve in your relationship, but you're scared that you're going to offend your partner by telling them:

When You Are Dealing With Criticism in Relationships:

1.   Ask if you don't understand 100 percent of the criticism; your partner might say one thing, and you might hear another. Give them a chance to explain what they mean; it could differ completely from what you heard the first time around!

2.   Remind yourself that this is not a criticism of you as a human being, but of part of your actions.

3.   Remind yourself that this is just a personal opinion.

4.   Accept whatever you've been criticized for, and think about it if you will want to change it; is that something you agree with?

At sometimes, you need to acknowledge the behaviors or views you don't like about your partner. Accepting your partner's imperfections and character flaws is a fundamental part of loving your partner and developing a strong bond.

Good relationships are also based on getting closer to your partner and trying to find compromises that both of you can handle.

However, when you compromise on something, you need to make sure that neither of you is trying to achieve something impossible, nor that one or both of you will likely end up profoundly disappointed and unhappy.

If you change the basic parts of yourself to appease your partner, you will end up relying on your self-esteem and affirmation, a burden that no partner can bear in the long term.

It would make sense to change yourself, after all, your partner is the initiator, because you've already been thinking about it yourself – i.e., you're setting his/her goal, your goal.

Some Thoughts on Constructive Criticism

If anything worries you enough about your partner that has a negative effect on you, it's important to tell your partner about it. Otherwise, your frustration and disappointment will cause a rift between the two of you that your partner might not even be aware of or know the cause.

Try to tell your partner precisely what bothers you and let them know that you're telling them because you love him/her, and you're doing it because your relationship and your partner are essential to you.

Enable your partner to get upset, frustrated, or hurt. You don't have the power to keep that from happening, so it's only normal for your partner to show frustration after finding out that something is going to make you unhappy.

The Art of Criticizing and Getting Rid of the Bad Feelings Successfully

How can I tell her that when she comes home late, she's driving me nuts? That he's supposed to wash his dishes without having to ask him every time? I hate it when he smokes when I eat? It bothers me too much when she interrupts me when I talk to someone else?

We always find ourselves in circumstances where we want to blame our partner because he or she does or does something that annoys and upsets us.

You know what you want to say, but you might be afraid of your partner's reaction, that he or she would take it as an insult and be hurt and resentful.

You want to tell them how you feel, but fear it's going to come out as rude and negative (remember, when I say criticism, I'm talking positive, not hurtful).

Try it as you might, you don't know how your partner would react to your criticism. You can't know or anticipate how your partner would take it, so you need to be mindful that no one likes to be criticized, even though you're trying to be supportive.

But and this is a big 'but,' criticism is necessary, whether you like it or not. Without suggestions about doing something "wrong" or something out of reach, you and your partner won't be able to grow further as a couple and move past things that bother you.

Chapter 6.   Trust Your Partner

There are many ideas out there about what makes a relationship work. Some say passion; some say commitment. As you go through these questions and give your spouse the honest truth, it should become apparent that what makes a marriage work is the same thing that makes any relationship work: trust.

Of course, trust and commitment have much in common. The first exercise I want you and your partner to do is define trust together. Ask yourselves what trust means for you, and what it means for your relationship.

After doing this exercise, it should be easier to figure out what the difference between commitment and trust is. As defined in dialectical behavior therapy, commitment is the action we take to stay with our spouse through thick and thin. Trust is the reason we commit to them — whether those reasons are emotional, practical, or from our experiences with them.

The big difference between a marriage and a relationship is that you need to be there for each other in almost every aspect of your lives. That's why the strength of your trust must be much greater than for any other relationship. Even the smallest hint of doubt in your trust for your spouse has remarkable consequences.

Commitment is less of a problem when you falter on it from time to time. All of us are human, so sometimes we do not act as though we are as committed to the relationship as we should be. This is normal, and it does not mean we are not taking the relationship seriously.

Falling below a certain threshold with our trust in our spouse is a different story. We don't have the option to place little trust in them, because we are relying on them.

When we feel we can't rely on the one person we should be able to rely on, it leads to some real problems. A relationship where one partner doesn't trust the other, or where neither partner trusts the other, will not last.

There is a physical component to trust, too. Although the bulk of this book concerns itself with the emotional and psychological dimensions of relationships, the sexual, sensual, and romantic dimensions are not something you can ignore.

It depends on your specific relationship, too. You might be the kind of couple that falls back on sexual trust to reaffirm your trust in other areas of life. Alternatively, you might treat it as an entirely separate issue.

Both ways are valid, and this is why I had you objectively determine what kind of couple you were at the beginning of the workbook.

Trust doesn't have to be static. It is something that can come and go. You might think you trust someone at first, but then you learn more about them, and you don't trust them anymore.

It is the same way in relationships. Maybe you want to trust your spouse — or you want them to trust you — but something happens that led to your trust in each other diminishing. There are actionable steps you can take to make your trust in each other go back up.

The first is to make your words meaningful. Part of this is telling the truth and not lying. When you find out your partner lies a lot, it becomes incredibly challenging to think anything they say means anything. You start to question everything they say, even if they aren't lying anymore.

This problem will eventually occur in every relationship. If your partner has been lying to you, why would you believe anything they say to you? The truth is, they have lied before. After having been in an abusive relationship for a while, your subconscious brain has a lot of emotional and logical problems when it comes to handling being lied to.

If your partner has never lied to you before, it is most likely a sign that they are a great person and are highly capable of being a good father.

If you used to lie and want to recover your relationship from that phase, you need to affirmatively tell your partner that you are dedicated to not lying anymore. Tell them that from this point on, you only say what you mean. Anything you say you mean.

I have talked a little bit about vulnerability throughout the book. Vulnerability is a huge component of trust.

It is basically the same in all relationships — not just romantic ones. People feel more willing to trust you when they feel like you are opening yourself up to them — when you are being vulnerable.

You may wonder why this would be the case. It's because when we trust someone to do something for us, we need to place some faith in them. It puts us in a vulnerable position ourselves when we trust someone because if they betray us, they could hurt us.

Therefore, when someone allows us to see their vulnerability, it makes us feel better in turn about being vulnerable with them. We become more willing to share our secrets with them and trust them.

With your spouse, try to open up about the things that bother you. Share your insecurities with them. By doing this, you will make them feel like they can trust you because you are being vulnerable with them.

There is another important way for you to regain trust from your partner: you have to give them the benefit of the doubt.

This is a theme that you may have noticed come up again and again in this workbook. You have to allow people to be better in order to let them improve. Constantly criticizing your partner for their past mistakes is justified on some level. However, if you want them ever to change, you need to keep these criticisms to yourself.

People become what we tell them they are. Telling your spouse that they are lazy will lead them to start seeing themselves as lazy. Then, they will start doing things that lazy people do. You will believe they were just lazy all along, and that your labeling them had nothing to do with it.

Trust isn't the same for everyone. There are personality types who are more trusting of others, while other personality types have issues trusting a single person. Even when we trust one person over everyone else, you still might not trust them completely.

I am not telling you and your spouse to put aside all doubts about your partner. What I am saying is that you will both make mistakes. Some of them very big.

Even when this happens, though, you have to keep on trusting your spouse. The trust you have in them should not come from the fact that they are perfect every day, but from that, your spouse tries to be better every day. When they are demonstrating to you that they want to be better for you, you should be open to trusting them.

Chapter 7.   Revive Your Sex Life

For many couples, issues arising in the bedroom can lead to deeper problems within the relationship. If you and your partner struggle to be sexually intimate, these problems can spill over into other areas of your life, causing a breakdown in connection at all levels.

While of course there are no set guidelines as to how often you and your partner should be having sex – some couples happily go months or even years without while others require it every day – it is important to address any issues surrounding sexual intimacy as early as possible.

Like many things in life, it is the quality of your sexual connection that matters, not how often you engage in intercourse. Employing some of the techniques below can assist you in creating a deeper connection with your partner – both physical and emotionally – leading to a better sex life, and a deeper connection on all levels.

Maintain Physical Contact and Affection

Maintaining physical contact with your partner throughout the day is a key way to ensure the spark remains alive. This can be as simple as a quick kiss, a gentle hand on the back, or a hug. It's the simple act of making contact that shows your partner you love them and find them attractive.

Educate Yourself

In today's information age, there is no shortage of material both on and offline covering just about every sexual issue you can think of. Find some resources that apply to your particular situation, sharing them with your partner. While it's great to be able to discuss this openly, many couples find this difficult to do. Alternatively, consider highlighting or underlining passages you find relevant, then sharing the reference with your partner. This can be an important first step in opening up dialogue around your sex life.

If openly discussing your sex life with your partner is a challenge for you, it can be helpful to consider why. Is it a matter of not trusting your partner enough, or has your upbringing lead you to believe that sexuality is not something that should be tackled openly? Whatever the reason, identifying the reason behind your reluctance can be an important first step to overcoming it.

Make Time for Sex

When the busyness of life overwhelms us, our sex lives often get neglected. And while it may sound unromantic, scheduling time for sex ensures it does not slip off the radar. This is particularly important if you have children who take up the majority of your time, or if you are getting older, when your sexual responses typically slow down and being intimate with your partner may require more time.

Discuss Your Sexual Fantasies

If you and your partner are able to talk openly about sex, it does not just mean you'll be more fulfilled in the bedroom. It means you are deeply connected and much more able to be open with each other in every aspect of your lives. After all, our sexual fantasies are one of the most personal aspects of ourselves, and when we trust someone enough to share them, it lets them know we have the utmost faith in them. Talking openly with your partner about your sexual fantasies lays the groundwork for deeper trust and openness, not to mention a more exciting sex life.

Communicate During Sex

This does not necessarily mean engaging in dirty talk – although if that's your thing, great. Rather, it's about improving your levels of intimacy by giving your partner cues to have sex more pleasurable for both of you. These could be verbal cues, or simple instructions, or even just the act of guiding your partner's hands. As close as you are, you cannot expect your partner to read your mind – and letting your partner know exactly what turns you on will make the experience more memorable for both of you.

Relax

Particularly if you and your partner have been having issues in the bedroom, sex can become a stressful event. To relieve anxiety, be sure to engage a relaxing activity beforehand. This could include going out for dinner, doing yoga, meditation or deep breathing exercises, or even just giving each other a back rub. The activity itself it not important; it's all about ensuring that when you make it to bed, you have no anxiety or concerns about what is about to happen.

Practice the Sensate Focus Technique.

A technique widely used by sex therapists, Sensate Focus is used to help increase people's enjoyment of sex, while deepening their connection to their partner. It operates on the basis of "mindful sex," helping people get out of their heads in order to enjoy their body fully. As much of the technique actually prohibits the touching of the breasts and genitals, Sensate Focus is far more about awakening one's sensuality, rather than their sexuality – in turn, deepening their connection to both their own body, and their partner.

To begin, decide which of you will be the "toucher" and who will be the "receiver." Take a shower beforehand and remove your clothes, along with any watches or jewelry. Find a time and place where you will not be interrupted. If you have been designated the "receiver" find a position in which you can lie down comfortably. If you are the "toucher," spend at least fifteen minutes exploring your partner's body, avoiding the genitals and breasts. Pay attention to how the texture of his or her skin changes in different parts of the body. Compare the skin on the back of the arm, for example, to the skin on the cheek. Now, vary the tempo and pressure of your touch. How does this change your experience? Also try touching with different parts of your hand. Use one or two fingers for a while, then change to your palm, or the back of your hand. How does this change the experience? Note that the point here is not to arouse yourself or your partner, or to touch them in a way you think they will enjoy. It is simply an exercise in mindfulness and connecting with your own body, and that of your partner's.

Now change roles. As the "receiver," pay attention to the way each movement feels on your skin. How do the sensations change when your partner uses different speeds, or different parts of his/her hands to touch you? You may like to continue with this first step for several days, before moving on to the next part.

Step two involves the same mindfulness technique, this time allowing the touching of the breasts and genitals. Despite this, the aim is still mindfulness and awareness, rather than pleasure. As you implement this second step, you may find yourself instinctively drawn towards sexual touching. If that happens, slow down and return to the techniques used in step one; namely, focusing on the textures of your partner's body, and the different qualities of your touch. Don't focus on the touching of genitals – remember here the idea is not sexual contact, just a broader exploration.

At this point in the exercise you may choose to implement the "hand-riding technique" in which the receiver covers the toucher's hand with their own as he or she continues to explore their body. The aim here is not for the receiver to outwardly guide the toucher to where they want to be touched, but rather to impart any subtle non-verbal cues, such as where a heavier touch is welcome, or areas which are less or more sensitive. It's important to note here that the toucher should not interpret these cues as criticism, but rather as suggestions.

It is particularly important in this step to refrain from kissing, as this can lead into automatic sexual touching and responses, which is not the aim of this exercise. Often, kissing is a part of the old, routine sexual habits that the Sensate Focus technique aims to break.

Despite the fact that the goal here is not sexual touching, if the receiver finds themselves brought to orgasm, just let it happen; but do not aim for this outcome.

Like step one, you may wish to continue with this step for several days before moving on to the next one.

Step three removes the roles of "toucher" and "receiver" to allow for mutual sensual touching. The same rules apply as for step two – you may touch any area of your partner's body, though the goal is sensual exploration, rather than giving or receiving sexual pleasure. Continue to refrain from kissing.

If the routine nature of your sex life is something you are trying to break, consider doing this step in a location other than your bed, such as the shower, or living room, if you live alone.

Step four progresses to the act of sensual – not sexual – intercourse. Just as you did in step three, take time to enjoy the textures and shapes of each other's bodies, without having any particular goal in mind. From here, move to a position in which intercourse is physically possible. If you don't wish to engage in intercourse at this time, that's absolutely fine; simply continue with the sensual exploration of each other's bodies. But if you do wish to progress, be sure to do so in a slow and mindful way, taking note of the physical sensations and ensuring you remain in your body, not allowing your mind to drift, or to engage in sexual fantasies. Keep your focus on the sensations throughout, remembering that the goal here is simply to be present and mindful, not necessarily to reach orgasm.

The Sensate Focus technique is a method you can return to from time to time in order to break up any monotony in your sex life.

Chapter 8.   Love

It is love that binds the couple. In fact, the act of effective communication is a manifestation of love where you share your thoughts and emotions with each other. This is trust, knowing that there is no guarantee that your spouse will not break your heart in the future. In the same way, you also spend the time to listen to him/her not because you have read about effective communication, but because you love him so much that you want to spend your precious time hearing his voice and knowing his thoughts and feelings.

Even when all else fails, love can set things right. In fact, it is the love that you have for your spouse that will lead you to have a better bond and improved communication. Just the fact that you are reading this book right now only proves that you do love your spouse and that you are willing to take positive actions to make your relationship work. No matter how your relationship is doing right now, know that you can always make it last, as long as you truly love each other.

Love is the power that binds your marriage, and it is also what connects you to each other. If there is one important thing that you should remember from this book, that is to love your spouse with all your heart. When you do, then all the techniques in this book will come to you easily and naturally. If you just examine the techniques written in this book, you will recognize that they are all acts of love.

This book only reminds you of how to be a lover. In modern time, it is quite easy to forget what it really means to love a person. Unfortunately, there are now so many preconceptions and ideas of how loving another should be, that people have forgotten what love really means.

If there is something truly valuable in the world, then that is love. It is love that keeps you together and connects you to each other. Without love, no marriage will ever work regardless of how many communication techniques that you apply. But, if you have love, and if you give it enough time to express itself, then you will even find out other ways to improve your communication.

The power of love is beyond any technique of communication. However, love cannot be forced. There is no way that you can have quality time with someone whom you do not even love. But, if you truly love your spouse, then you have a very good chance of making your marriage work. Communication is also an act of love. This is another reason why you should improve your level of communication in your marriage. As you may already know, couples with poor communication are usually the ones who do not last long. When communication fails, love follows.

But the interesting news is that there is something that you can do about this. With your love for your spouse, you can turn a problematic relationship into a marriage that is full of love, kindness, and understanding. After all, love is a powerful force that can move mountains. Love is the key.

Use Affirmations

While displaying love in your marriage, you should also learn the use of affirmations. Affirmations are words and acts that affirm your love for each other. When last did you tell your spouse that you love him or her? When was the last time you bought him a gift to show how you appreciate and love him? Marriage is like a flower that you water every day for it to bloom and grow.

In the same way, you should affirm for each other regularly. It is not enough that your spouse knows that you love him. You should also make him or her feel it. Fortunately, there are more than a thousand ways to express one's love for another. Over the years that you will spend together as a couple, you will definitely not run out of ways to show your love and make your spouse feel it more deeply.

Affirming one's love is done by continuously loving your spouse. There are many ways to affirm your love, whether through your words or deeds. Never forget to tell your spouse that he or she is important to you.

Avoid saying "I love you." as a mere habit. Those are three sacred and powerful words that deserve attention and respect. Say "I love you" because you mean it and say it as you look straight into your beloved's eyes.

Affirming one's love should not be seen as a duty or obligation. After all, if you are truly in love with your spouse, then affirming your love for him or her would be a natural expression of yourself. Also, you will never run out of ways to affirm your love. It can be as simple as cooking his favorite dishes, buying a surprise gift, among many others. It can also be a surprise dinner date at some luxurious restaurant, a special trip for a vacation, etc. There is no limit to how you can affirm your love for your spouse because love is infinite.

The use of kind words when you give compliments is one of the best ways to express love. When you do this, be sure that you also use the right tone of voice. Words alone are nothing — you also need to be sincere. If you are sincere enough, and if you express your message the right way, then your spouse would feel it.

Affirming your love to your spouse is something that you should continuously do without an end. If you truly love your spouse, then this is something that is very easy and natural to do. People who are in love usually affirm their love even without thinking about it. Unfortunately, during the long course of a marriage and because of the demands of modern life, you may have to remind yourself every now and then to do some positive action to affirm your love to your spouse. This is good, and you should turn this into a habit. Make sure to affirm your love at least once every week.

Make Your Spouse Feel Important

Right now, it should be clear to you that your spouse is one of the most important people in the world for you. It is only right that you let him or her know how important he or she is in your life. There are several ways to do this. You can use words and tell him or her just how important he or she is to you and you can also express it through your actions. You can get him a gift, write him a letter, give him a message, or simply treat him in a special way.

If you think that your spouse might not completely understand your kind gesture of love, then use words to make it very clear to him or her. The important thing is to make sure that him or her knows and feels that he or she is important in your life.

When a person is treated in a special way, it makes him feel important. It makes him feel loved. Hence, making your spouse feel important can-do wonders for a relationship. Now, if it is your spouse who makes a move to make you feel just how important you are, make sure to express your appreciation. Although this is not related directly to communication, take note that improving the relationship can also improve the level of communication.

Another way to show your spouse just how important he is to you is by listening to him when he talks. A simple example of this is to stop whatever it is that you are doing when he talks to you. Of course, if you are the man, you should also do the same. These days, many couples do not talk properly. It is not uncommon to find couples who talk while the other person is watching a movie or reading a book.

They fail to give 100% of their attention to each other. Yes, you can still engage in conversation and be responsive even while doing something else, but the point here is that you are not giving your spouse your full attention, and this does not make your spouse feel important. You should treat your spouse in a special way.

When you communicate with your spouse, it is always worth reminding yourself that you are talking to the most important person in your life. Unfortunately, many people fail to realize the value of their spouse and take every moment that they share together for granted. Make every moment count. Focus on your spouse and always treat him or her in a very special way.

Now, it is not uncommon for people to feel that they are probably no longer important to their spouse. This is true, especially when your spouse is so busy with work and other obligations that he or she has no time to enjoy life with you — and this is also wrong. Unfortunately, this has become common in many marriages these days.

However, you should not let something like this to continue. If you feel like you are in this situation, then you should talk to your spouse about it. Another effective way is to be the one to show to your spouse just how important he is to you. You do not have to make things complicated or suffer in silence. Do not forget that your spouse is there for you. If you are not happy about something in your relationship, then face it together as a team.

It is noteworthy that making your spouse feel important takes positive actions on your part. Do not be content with just knowing that he or she is important to you, but you should communicate this message through your actions and in a way that will make him or her feel just how truly important he or she is in your life.

Chapter 9.   Accept Your Partner

In any relationship, we need to be able to accept our partners the way they are no one is perfect and an important thing to remember is that perfection is a myth. No one in this world is perfect, and everyone is flawed. If you come into your relationship thinking that your partner is perfect and that you won't have any issues then this you are setting yourself up for very unrealistic expectations, it's because they didn't realize that chasing perfection doesn't get you anywhere. Instead of trying to make everything perfect, accept your partner how they are, and love them unconditionally.

When we decide to share our life with someone else we've already taken the time to get to know them, and we take the time to understand who they are and what they're about when we take the step to join our lives with them forever we have told them that we accept them for who they are Is after you have gotten in a relationship you find that this is not true anymore than your relationship needs work a relationship cannot work if you do not accept your partner for who they are By that same logic by that same logic your partner and yourself will have bed communication and find that you're unable to communicate as efficiently as you'd like to because you feel that your partner doesn't understand you which can lead to feelings of neglect.

Remember that you don't want your partner to have unrealistic expectations of you so you shouldn't have unrealistic expectations for them either. If you want your relationship to work, then you will need to understand the importance of being able to make sure that you are thinking realistically.

When you become frustrated with your partner, you need to pull back and recognize what it is you're thinking. Is what you are thinking something that your partner really needs to change or is it something that you've built up in your mind because you have unrealistic expectations about what they should be or what you want them to be? Is it something that you need to change with your thought process, or is it something that genuinely needs to be changed in your partner himself? Another question that you should ask yourself is why is it your partner's job to live up to unrealistic expectations? On the opposite side to this, why is it your job to live up to your partner's unrealistic expectations? You need to realize that having the right expectations of yourself, your partner, and your relationship are the best ways that you're going to be able to make this relationship work.

Flexibility is another thing that is going to help you appreciate your partner and make sure that you are accepting them the way they are. It's very easy to think of the world as just black or just white and think that this is wrong, or this is right, and there is no in-between, but that's not realistic. Things don't have to be one way or the other. Instead of labeling your way as the right way or your partner's way is the right way, remember that you need to compromise and understand how things actually are.

Negative thinking is much easier for some people than positive thinking because being negative doesn't require half as much effort as being positive. When a person is being negative and thinking negatively, it's very self-imposed and self-centered behavior. When we think negatively, we are not accepting our partner for who they are, and instead, you see the negative in them because you're focusing on being negative yourself. Being positive instead of focusing on why your partner is the way that he is will cause you to be able to focus on what's amazing about him and why you like him in the first place. This, in turn, is going to lead you to accept him for who he is, and this will lead to you appreciating him for who he is as well. Just as you need the love of your partner to make you happy and whole, your partner needs your love to make him happy and whole as well. He needs you to be here for him as well.

Another helpful hint to appreciating your partner is to force yourself to see things in a different light and put the focus on you. What we mean by this is that you should ask yourself how you would feel if your partner was judging you the way that you're judging them. Another question you should ask is that if they didn't accept you the way that you're not accepting them how you would feel if you thought your partner didn't understand you or love you the way that you needed to be loved and respected? Keeping this in mind, you'll be much more flexible, and you'll be able to understand why you shouldn't treat your partner this way.

You should also strive to remember that the past is gone and there's nothing you can do about it. You can make up for the past. That part is possible, and we're not saying that it is not. What we're saying is whatever happened in the past you can't go back in time and make it so that that didn't happen. There are no do-overs or a reset button on the things you do because life is not a video game. It's here and now and you need to learn that if you make a mistake, you can't undo it, but you can try and fix it and move on from it. You just need to remember that whatever has happened has already happened and there's nothing you can do to change that. We all make mistakes, so instead of focusing on the past, try living in the present and give your partner the gift of understanding that. If you're always comparing things to how they were before or you're always comparing things to the past and bringing up past arguments along with things that can't be changed, the only thing that you are actually doing is hindering your acceptance of your partner and your acceptance of each other. If this continues over time, it could actually end up destroying your relationship because you're not focusing on the future the way that you need to be. The biggest reason that this is an issue that can be so damaging is because when you are doing this, it brings resentment and past pain to the relationship. This, in turn, brings hurt into the relationship, along with fighting and harsh words. To avoid this, you should focus on the present and what you can do in the present to change things to make them better for your partner and yourself.

When we judge others it's often a result of our own personal criticisms that we've had to endure ourselves, but we shouldn't put pressure on ourselves to do things a certain way, and we shouldn't put pressure on our partner to do things that way either. Letting what others have said to you or done to you can affect you and your thought process and the way you treat others, including your partner. This is why people say your past shapes who you are. If your mistreated when your younger or you've had bad relationships, you can unintentionally carry that over into your future relationships even though you don't mean to. The way to get past this is to understand that that is what you've got this issue in the first place and then work on trying to change. In the long run, this will ensure that your heart and spirit are happier and more fulfilled. This will cause your treatment of your partner to get better and make sure that your partner's spirit and heart are happier too.

When you put unnecessary pressure on your partner, the only thing you're doing is pushing them away. Now every relationship has pressure, and every relationship has areas where your partner will be under pressure but what we're saying is instead of judging yourself and judging others understand that everyone has limitations and you can't put too much pressure on someone because they will crack. This may not happen right away, especially if your partner is strong, but eventually, even the strongest person can break eventually if you keep pushing them too hard. If you cause your partner to crack, then your relationship is going to falter immediately because they're going to feel resentment towards you for doing so. When you are happy and fulfilled as an individual you will be less critical and rude to your partner.

Something to remember is that even though your partner can meet your needs, you can meet your own needs as well. You can also meet your partner's needs as they meet yours. In order to fully appreciate your partner and to accept them for who they are, you need to remember that when you are happy with yourself, you'll be happy with everything around you. The same is true if you're unhappy. If you are unhappy with everything around you, you are going to be overly critical of your partner, and you won't appreciate them for who they are.

When you recognize that you're unhappy, you will at least be able to understand that you need to tell your partner in a loving and respectful manner that you're unhappy. Then you can work together on becoming happier so that you can appreciate each other and accept each other the way you need to. Negativity in a relationship is one of the biggest reasons that a relationship can falter because when that happens, it breeds insecurity, painful arguments, and hurt in the relationship that you have. When you're able to understand that you and your partner can meet your needs and that you should apply positive thinking instead of negativity, you'll be able to see your partner as your partner.

This is what you should be seeing them as instead of just seeing your partner as someone who's supposed to meet every single need of yours.

Something to remember is that a happy relationship will occur when two people are happy and content. When two people are happy and content with coming together and being together, they realize that their relationship has fewer problems and they are much better at appreciating each other. Many people have heard the expression that their partner completes them, and for many, this is true. For just as many, they feel completely alone and love that that feeling grows with their partner. For many happy couples, they understand that they feel complete already with their partner and with themselves. So, they have the best of both worlds.

Each of us has to be responsible at least in part for our own happiness and because of this happy person in a relationship is able to increase the flexibility and the happiness that you have together as a couple in your relationship.

Chapter 10.   Communicate with Your Partner

Communication is absolutely necessary for your relationship to thrive. Without it, the love and fire in your relationship will grow cold and dead. Communication is like oxygen to a relationship. Most people think effective communication is all about merely listening actively, but there is so much more to it. It would also behoove you to realize that each gender communicates, differently because they see things differently.

Thanks to the science of psychology, we understand that the differences in communication between the genders are partly as a result of both genders being kept apart from each other while growing up. Since girls mostly hang out with girls and boys with boys due to societal norms and cultures, there can be a bit of disconnect in understanding the way the other gender processes stuff and communicates how they feel. It's almost always a case of little boys playing with trucks and little girls playing dress up or dolls.

Communication Is Not Just Verbal

Communication is not only verbal, however. It is also important to understand that non-verbal cues differ for both men and women. Of course, the facial expressions for a lot of situations will remain the same. Like the typical grimace when anyone, male or female, bites into a slice of lemon, as opposed to the smile that follows a bite of homemade lemon meringue pie.

There are seven types of non-verbal cues. Knowing how both genders use these cues will change the way you and your spouse communicate with each other for the better. This way, you can become more aware of your lover's goals, hopes, needs, and fears, with little or no misunderstanding. Let's take a look at what these non-verbal cues are.

Physical contact: Regardless of genetic makeup, males and females communicate very differently through touch. While for men heavy slaps on the back and rough nudges are a way to display camaraderie, power, influence, and dominance, women take the much gentler route of offering a hug or reaching out to pat the other person's shoulder to show compassion, or simply refraining from touch when not in the mood or angry or wronged in some way.

Thanks to science and a whole lot of research, we now know that touch causes the release of oxytocin, which automatically causes the couple sharing the touch to feel better about themselves and, in one another's company, no matter how terrible their days have gone. Sometimes it is not Advil you need, but a great big hug.

Facial Expressions

The human face is a wonder. There are 43 different facial muscles in the face, which are capable of a myriad of expressions — the closest and most recent estimate being approximately 10,000. This makes human facial expression one of the most important non-verbal ways we communicate.

More often than not, women use a lot of facial expressions. There is eye contact, or the lack of it. There's nodding the head, and pursing of the lips — a lot more compared to men. In addition to having a lot of facial expressions, women are often better at reading facial expressions, thanks to their intuitive and evocative nature. If you doubt this, try telling a lie to a female. For the most part, it won't take long until you're found out.

Paralinguistic Communication

Have you ever wondered why a word or sentence can imply several different things depending on the way it's said? If you have, then you either know of or have had some experience with a little something called paralinguistic communication.

Also called "para language," it is the study of voice, tone, and the various nuances and cues accompanying words when they are said. They represent aspects of communication that go beyond words. There are a bunch of things to consider when we speak of paralanguage, including fluency, pitch, accent, speech rate, and modulation. You've also got to keep track of cues like hand gestures, body language, eye movements, and the like.

Paralinguistic communication is important, as the more you understand it, the less likely people will be able to hide the truth and cover up emotions around you. This is a great thing, because once you know what the actual problem you're addressing with your spouse at any given point in time is, it's easier for you to address the actual issue, and not the secondary reason they give you.

Body Posture

Since men usually tend to command more personal space than the female folk, they are more likely to align their bodies in a such a way that their feet are more spaced apart, with their arms placed farther apart from their bodies when they are upset or feel challenged. Females, on the other hand, retract and keep their arms close together with their feet crossed when they feel intimidated, afraid, or averse to a particular person or situation.

You want to be careful when you're interpreting body language. Always pay attention to the context in which you observe it. Don't assume your wife is upset with you because she's hugging herself — it could just be really cold outside for her.

Causes of Miscommunication in a Relationship

The he versus she complexes: While women use communication as a means to build relationships and intimacy, men don't understand the logic behind using so many words. Many men are of the opinion that communication should have a clear goal and they see no use communicating if they are not allowed to fix anything.

If a woman tells her spouse about how she feels overweight and finds it difficult to lose the post baby weight, a typical male response would probably be along the lines of, "I have the number of a great personal trainer," or "Why don't you cut down on all those fries?" Now these comments may sound like an insult to her body image, but he genuinely feels he is offering advice. All the woman wants is to be told she is beautiful no matter what the scale reads.

Active or passive listening? It is a Herculean task to get most men to listen without wanting to chip in with a solution or their feelings about an issue. Another issue would probably be just how much to say in a given situation. Just how much is too much? Before a man answers a question or narrates an occurrence, he has sifted through the events in his own mind. In the end, he only winds up telling the aspects he feels are connected to the story.

The reverse is the case with the opposite gender. Women use the power of words to comprehend their experiences and emotions fully. There are times when a woman may not understand what she is feeling and why she feels that way, until after she has talked about it. This is why the worst thing you could possibly do is not respond when a woman is sharing her feelings and thoughts with you. You may assume you're paying attention and that should be enough, but that's not the case. You should show that you do indeed understand her, by putting yourself in her shoes and feeling what she feels, too.

These differences in communication would explain why a man becomes withdrawn and retreats to a spot where he feels safest (man cave, anyone?) This man cave serves as a mini vacation spot without the extra expenses incurred with tickets and such. In the safety of his own space, he sorts out his emotions, and tries to comprehend what he is feeling.

This period of withdrawal can leave his spouse wondering if she is at fault in some way or if she is losing him. That's not necessarily the case. Women, when confronted with a particularly tight or difficult situation, would value support and some level of care and nurturing from her significant other, as she would definitely use words to communicate and try to process her feelings.

Avoiding Misunderstandings

Now that the complex nature of communication has been established, and I have made it clear that gender differences only add to this complexity, I want to point out that all this does not mean men and women are incapable of getting along. They can. It's simply a matter of practice, and a willingness to understand one another.

The overall purpose of improving communication in your relationship or marriage is to adapt to one another's style of communication, rather than try to change the other person completely. Here are some facts you need to be aware of if you want to practice effective communication with your significant other:

1.   Recognize that communication has different and distinct styles and each have their strengths and weaknesses.

Understand these and don't be quick to find faults or point accusing fingers.

2.   Try not to fit into or feed the stereotypes that exists with gender differences. Understand that the environment plays a huge part in the way to respond verbally or nonverbally.

3.   Be aware and get information concerning the different communication styles in order to control your response to each one effectively. Recognize the different styles that exist and adapt fluidly to each one.

CONCLUSION

Narcissists do not even think about how their behavior affects others, and this is why they find it so easy to use emotionally abusive and manipulative techniques in their relationships. Narcissists operate in romantic relationships; it exposes the words they say and the actions they take to abuse victims. Also, empowering strategies as to how to disarm narcissists and how to deal with narcissism in dating have been explained. With the proper management techniques, any victim can get over the emotional abuse and mental manipulation of dating or being involved with a narcissist to go on and lead a productive and fulfilling life. It is usual for victims of abuse to cry after their ordeal and think whatever went wrong with the relationship was their fault, which is what the narcissist wanted; a traumatic experience for the victim The narcissist is a real-life zombie. Rather than feast on flesh, they feast on you, your compassion, empathy, frustration, stress, and anything adverse they can get you to feel. The narcissist will never change, no matter how long suffering or persevering you are. This is something I keep repeating over and over, because they will promise you, they can change. In fact, they will show signs of improvement! But in the end, it's all a game. They just want to lull you into a false sense of safety and security. They just want to take you even higher up the mountain so that they can dash you and your hopes harder against the rocks in the valley even more devastatingly than they did the last time.

Try to understand that as far as the narcissist is concerned, you exist purely for entertainment purposes.

CPSIA information can be obtained
at www.ICGtesting.com
Printed in the USA
BVHW090943030621
608731BV00010B/1949